D0994371

The Beautiful Librarians

SEAN O'BRIEN is a poet, critic, playwright,
broadcaster, anthologist and editor. He grew up in Hull
and now lives in Newcastle upon Tyne; he is Professor of
Creative Writing at Newcastle University and Fellow of the
Royal Society of Literature. *The Drowned Book* won both the
Forward Prize for best collection and the T. S. Eliot Prize.
His most recent collection, *November*, was shortlisted
for the Costa Poetry Award, the T. S. Eliot Prize,
the Forward Prize and the International
Griffin Poetry Prize.

Sean O'Brien

The Beautiful Librarians

PICADOR

First published 2015 by Picador
an imprint of Pan Macmillan, a division of Macmillan Publishers Limited
Pan Macmillan, 20 New Wharf Road, London N1 9RR
Basingstoke and Oxford
Associated companies throughout the world
www.panmacmillan.com

ISBN 978-1-4472-8751-3

Copyright © Sean O'Brien 2015

The right of Sean O'Brien to be identified as the
author of this work has been asserted by him in accordance
with the Copyright, Designs and Patents Act 1988.

All rights reserved. No part of this publication may be reproduced,
stored in a retrieval system, or transmitted, in any form, or by any means
(electronic, mechanical, photocopying, recording or otherwise)
without the prior written permission of the publisher.

1 3 5 7 9 8 6 4 2

A CIP catalogue record for this book is available from the British Library.

Printed and bound by CPI Group (UK) Ltd, Croydon, CR0 4YY

This book is sold subject to the condition that it shall not, by way of
trade or otherwise, be lent, hired out, or otherwise circulated without
the publisher's prior consent in any form of binding or cover other than
that in which it is published and without a similar condition including
this condition being imposed on the subsequent purchaser.

Visit **www.picador.com** to read more about all our books
and to buy them. You will also find features, author interviews and
news of any author events, and you can sign up for e-newsletters
so that you're always first to hear about our new releases.

to Alistair Elliot

ACKNOWLEDGEMENTS

BBC Radio 3, BBC Radio 4,
The Arts of Peace, Best British Poetry 2013,
The Best of Poetry London, B O D Y, Catch Up, Edinburgh Review,
The Guardian, Island, Jubilee Lines, Manchester Review, Matter,
Mutual Friends, NCLA, *New Humanist, New Yorker,*
The North, Northern Stage, *The Picador Book of 40,*
Poem, Poetry London, The Third Shore,
Times Literary Supplement.

Contents

The Beautiful Librarians

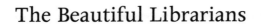

Audiology

I hear an elevator sweating in New Orleans,
Water folding black on black in tanks deep under Carthage,
Unfracked oil in Lancashire
And what you're thinking. It's the truth –
There goes your silent count to ten, the held breath
Of forbearance, all the language not yet spoken
Or unspeakable, the dark side of the page.
But this is not about you. I can hear
The sea drawn back from Honshu,
Hookers in the holding pen, and logorrhoea
In the dreaded Quiet Coach,
The firestorm of random signs
On market indices, the bull, the bear,
The sound of one hand clapping and the failure of the rains,
The crackle of the dried-out stars,
Stars being born, anomalies and either/or,
The soundtrack of creation in an unrecorded vowel,
The latest that might be the last, the leading edge
Of all that is the case or is not there.
'The contradictions cover such a range.'
And I'm told that soon it will be easier
To balance out the love-cry and the howl,
To wear an aid and act my age, to hear the world
Behind this world and not to crave amnesia.

Always

After Ruth Stone, 'Train Ride'

The morning lasts forever. It does not.
The teller in the high white room
Beside the silent harbour loathes
His ledgers and his counterfoils
But adds and checks and enters, does
What he is here to do. He knows the rules.
The sunlight floods a rubbled alleyway.
Venetians, Turks and all the rest
Are dead and gone, likewise their gold.
The enemy has sailed away,
Gone south, gone west,
But no one living has been told.
The morning is eternal. It is not.
For now is noon, the sun too hot
For thinking or for loving,
The noonday girl's asleep, her bitter breath
Distressing to the bitter clerk who lies
Beside her in the sunstruck heat, his cock
Shrunk back in white surrender.
Slowly in the blazing bay,
The ferry turns, is leaving.
The bank is opening again. The clock
Repeats that this is always, always,
That you are not here to wonder.

The hills grow pale. The sea's dim haze
Means time has passed invisibly again.
The widow in her blinding black
Comes up the street with bread and oil
And speaks to no one, and the surf
Returns, returns along the shore,
Still seeking the perfection of its form,
A girl not quite a girl, who frets through
Every finical frou-frou adjustment: *or*
Like this, perhaps, or this, or this,
Her breath still bitter in the kiss.
A sailor would know how to name that star,
The first of evening, hanging in the square.
Lock up the money and the bonds,
Remembering to wash your hands,
And let the world become anonymous.
In this day there are all the days.

Immortals

The Lodge, near Aviemore

At five the day begins a slow withdrawal
From the mountain valley and the silver roar
Of all its urgent streams. As dark comes on,
The sky and the snow in the forest
Are not grey but *gray*, American gray,
Like inbred Appalachian riflemen
Left lying where they fell along the Bloody Brook.

Up at the lodge, it is too late for us.
We linger in the library over tea
Beneath the photographs of OTCs
And smoke-shadowed portraits of womenfolk,
Shrivelled and crazed since they joined the firm.
All they have left are the hooks on their backs,
But we're the ones who are invisible.

For this is home to a confederacy. Their dead
Will not lie down, not even for the afternoon.
They have to own the air along the corridors,
And in the dining-hall beneath the snow-gray dome
And even outside on the snow-covered terrace
Where wrought-iron tables and chairs provide
Both audience and cast for a Chekhovian promenade.

– Grandmother, when shall we see Edinburgh again?
– Not in my lifetime, child, and I shall never die,
Not while the world affords me lace and bombazine.
There is no other world but ours, and those
Unlike ourselves are only servants in disguise.
Slaves and cotton, sugar and rum,
Turn the globe till Kingdom Come.

Another Country

'Get there if you can'
Auden

Scattered comrades, now remember: someone stole the staffroom tin
Where we collected for the miners, for the strike they couldn't win,

Someone stole a tenner, tops, and then went smirkingly away.
Whoever did it, we have wished you thirsty evil to this day:

You stand for everything there was to loathe about the South –
The avarice, the snobbery, the ever-sneering mouth,

The lack of solidarity with any cause but *me*,
The certainty that what you were was what the world should be.

The North? Another country. No one you knew ever went.
(Betteshanger, Snowdown, Tilmanstone: where were they? In Kent.)

'People' tell us nowadays these views are terribly unfair,
But these forgiving 'people' aren't the 'people' who were there.

Meanwhile your greying children smile and shrug: *That's history.*
So what's the point of these laments for how things used to be?

Whenever someone sagely says it's time to draw a line,
We may infer that they've extracted all the silver from the mine.

Where all year long the battle raged, there's 'landscape' and a plaque,
But though you bury stuff forever, it keeps on coming back:

Here then lie the casualties of one more English Civil War,
That someone, sometime – you, perhaps – will have to answer for.

Oysterity

Blah of the big society
And what we should give back —
The matter just kept coming up
All evening at the table:
A lot to swallow while we spoke
Of national austerity,
Of Cameron and Cable
And the coalition-claque.
So is it better out than in?
Purge the nation till it bokes
And purge us all of sin?
We went in for the oysters
We might never eat again,
Went for snot and shell-clack
As something to remember
In the times when fare is plainer:
The day will come when you no longer
Cash your cheques at Coutts.
Eat, be merry, sympathize,
But meanwhile fill your boots.
The truth hates a dissembler.
Then and there, what could we do?
It seemed like a no-brainer.
So we set about the oysters
In an orgy of the vowels,
Giving no thought to the morrow
Nor any to the bowels.

We were the slaves of history
But we ate in affirmation –
Bear the glut of privilege
Then stand with the protesters.
And write about it later –
Ah, the pleasures of the text.
You're a poet, you're a prophet,
You're out there on the edge,
You're all imagination
So you know what's coming next.
In the middle of the night
I knew I must return my share
To the stripped bed of the sea –
My long-term contribution
To sustainability.
I took the long view of the sink
Which was taking it from me –
Rose madder of unknown origin
Among the usual stuff.
I had to work to clear its gaze:
But it would neither wink nor blink.
Whatever I'd been served,
It left me badger-rough,
Eye-deep among the heaving stink,
Crouching, eyeing narrowly
The sink's own non-committal eye.
What did it mean? Just then it meant
I'd got what I deserved,
And all in all I'd rather die
Than go on paying back

The bellyful of slime
And glop and bladderwrack
It seemed I had ingested
With the spiced-up Amble oysters.
This government would make you sick!
I'd heard a neighbour say.
He took a glug of oyster, adding:
Their recipe's untested.
They've got us eating cack.
I took his point, for there was much
Too much to take in then and there,
So much that should, but as it proved,
Could never be digested.
Perhaps if I had cut my throat,
For in my guts I felt that's what
These policies suggested,
I should have spared myself the pain
Of picking through my entrails,
Learning that what's true for one
Who's disembowelled, disinvested,
Is also true for nations –
All remedies are poisonous
And even nations fail.
The oyster's aphrodisiac
May also steal your thunder.
Such ambiguous creations!
Then be charitable: give
A bit back when you chunder.
Anyway, I've had it now
With molluscs, and with seaweed
And with overpriced crustaceans.

Pedagogy

For Cynthia Fuller

Those dim white corridors that would be damp
Should their stern chatelaines
Ever cease to pay attention,
Where the smells of veg and polish meet,
Those sites of virtuous curiosity
With tea urns and plastic tablecloths
And warnings about washing up and folding chairs,
With Wordsworth, Mill and *Middlemarch*,
And a caretaker fretting
To get to the Legion by nine,
How could they be permitted to survive?

Or the library sheltering the indigent and mad
Among the adult categories,
Poetry, Fiction, History – clearly it became
Intolerable to any sane assessment,
Like the names of persons, places, things,
The dates, the spellings and the naïve rationale
That made them public. What can we
Have been thinking of, we dead,
In our sensible shoes, with our fussed-over folders
And mild, unprofitable passions? No? No answer?
Well, then, moving on –

2. The Seer

Dear friends, applaud the man's divine aplomb:
Today the seer says the time has come
To privatize the Somme and Passchendaele –
And if that works, then everything's for sale:

The eighteenth century? Keep out. Enclose
Old, wasteful, state-run epochs and let those
With money and imagination set
The idle dead to work, lest they forget –

For too long coddled by oblivion –
Which side their stones are buttered on.
The grave will cease to be a gravy-train,

At least for them. Think what we stand to gain,
The seer says, for no one ever lost
On Nagasaki or the Holocaust.

Infantry

We sing true North, deep North,
The north inside the air and underneath.
We come from it and vanish into it.
Fog, smoke, rain, the swags of hanging gas, they are all one to us.
We made this rain our own,
Picking for nuts on the sands of the coal coast,
Dining from tins at the pier-end in smeasling rain,
Drawn up like a squadron of tinplate armour
Across the glacis of a pit-site,
Facing the sea that calls to us
With gifts of rain and sandy mouthfuls.
We were deserted, and who
Do we serve as our boxes go by?
We were a moat defensive to a house we'll never own,
The parchment rotten in our mouths,
The pennies on our eyes gone copper-green.
We were a band of brothers,
Our courage signed over to sentiment
When once we'd made our marks
To show assent, we
The born soldiers, leaders of ditches,
Tommy this and Bobby that.
Where there was death we went
To mend it move it put it to the sword.
And Jimmy where's your legs?
Took off sir in the ditch at Skinningrove,
The ditch at Pity Me, at Nent,

At Wall and Oterborne and Flodden,
Paid off with the smeasling rain, the slick cold
In the sunk ditch, the syke —
His wife wepeth for him and siketh sore.
Then afterwards we come at dusk
Like starlings at the birchwood's edge,
Stooping in our greasy jerkins
To pick the dead over, to turn up
Our staring faces in the clotted ditch.
Then we suffer in turn, the histories say —
Caught out in enfilade on the glacis,
Encircled on the ravelin,
We stuck to our trades, as sapper, spark, mechanic,
Guarding the mamelon we'll never suck from,
Left to our songs and the names of our places of service and death,
The great ditch and the small, the syke, the soakaway.
We lie down, we lie down, in the ditch.
We are a river to our people,
Flowing, flowing, under the rain we become.

*

To be the servants of necessity,
Brunt-takers, those who have to understand
That this is more of that,
The same old shit, the facts, regrettably, regrettably.
To have no purchase on the voice
On which the facts can gain no purchase,
For the voice is money's voice
And money's not at home to us.
To be the ones that get the blame

In any case, for what we never did.
Is that a mystery, Sergeant? – Quiet now.
Blamed for being there, indeed
For being blamed (*oh cruel but fair*),
Oh, photographed in wordless lamentation
Waiting for a bus (*losers, losers*).
While purchase purchases elsewhere
We shall just be here anyway
Out on the field between the flats
For the whole white afternoon,
Our dogs like razors and our language worn away
To wordless shouts from an enormous distance.
Our array is much reduced
By plague and time's attrition,
The warhorse to the knacker's gone
And all his laughter took.

*

Let us be up long before the dawn –
Sunk Island and Spurn Point and Filey Brigg –
When men would go fishing, or walking the dog
And lovers walk each other shyly,
We come to the sea's edge, finding the way –
Marske and Saltburn, Redcar and Seaton Carew –
Out through the woods where no way is
And down through the wire and sea-grass
And past the immortal emplacements
Hard and good when we're decayed
What kind of lad was Jack the Lad? Why Jack's a soldier
Seaham and Roker, Shields and Shields

Cullercoats, St Mary's, Blyth and Low Newton
Craster and Beadnell and Seahouses
Follow the causeway out to the island,
The village sunk up to its knees in the sand,
To the graveyard at the sea's edge,
And down the narrow ditch and in
Through the steel door that shuts just the once,
On down the coal-road deep under the whale-road
(*Close order and still bloody raining*)
We sing true North, deep North
Until we are a song known only to the few,
And purchased by no one, an air
Behind the air, immortal and unheard.

War Graves

We were due here yesterday or never.
The dogs put up no birds, the rain goes over
And returns in almost-silence, filling in

The blanks among the beech and cypresses.
High summer in the empty hills, the cloud-armadas
Setting out and setting out, as though to promulgate

Epochal undertakings made elsewhere,
Whose impact scarcely registers
Among the stonecrop on the graveyard wall

Or on the shy memorial to Monkman, Bee and Bates
Who lived and died for this dispersed estate
Among these fields or at the Menin Gate.

Unending noon. The harvesters 'are stalled
Like tanks on the escarpment'. Must this be
'The trap of elegy', to find ourselves composed

Entirely of literature? To have no exit
From the immortality that holds us
Sheltering here beneath the canopy of beech

To wait the shower out inside the scent of earth and heat
And then pass through, an ignorant posterity
That cannot seal the yawning grave, still less survive it?

Damn Right I Got the Blues: Ovid Live in Tomis

1.

I hate to see that Euxine sun go down
I hate to see that Euxine sun go down
Cause Lord it reminds me that for reasons of state
I been exiled and confined to this one-horse Pontic town

2.

Ain't but one way out Caesar, but I just can't go out the door
Ain't but one way out Caesar, from this cell-block on the shore
Waited ten years for your letter, Oh Lord I'm waiting still
Barbarians don't get me then the ennui surely will

Jardin des Plantes

The ruined summer's lush despondency,
Arrested, Tennysonian . . . Late afternoon.
The bosom of the garden goddess runs
With freezing sweat, beneath the pale-pink
Blossom's rush to spend itself
On all this drowning air.
You'd give her one, you say. I doubt it.
We sit out on the sodden benches,
Stunned and half-asleep, like travellers
Abandoned by the railways
To a doomed domestic pastoral
Whose story lies elsewhere.
We are the disease that has no cure
Or visible employment. You, sir,
Call this contemplation: I call you
A wanker. If this place had
A yard-arm, the extinguished sun
Would hang itself. More rain.
The vindicated frogs carouse
And fuck. What time is it?

Thirteen O'Clocks

Grey days, a late spring, and in theory
The administration falls
With a commonsense rattle
Of handed-back car-keys,
Grey days when 'ideology',
The stuff that forms the very walls
On which the roof has always rested,
Unfolds like origami in reverse
To leave a bare white page
Uncannily like 'ideology'.
Essayists stand at their windows. Uh.
Meanwhile no blood and no curfew,
No lamp-posts. Life could be worse.

*

Parks and Gardens, Ways and Means,
Drains, Finance and General Purposes
And all the virtuous tedium required
To underwrite the civil surfaces,
The lawns on which the lovers lie
As bands complacently reiterate
The glories of our blood and state:
It takes a backfire (was it?) from a car
To call to mind that where we are
Is only happenstance and not
The happy land that history forgot.
See where an aged theorist takes the air.
Another car backfires. Christ, it's hot.

*

The tidal range is almost nil. Deep gulfs
Far out, but at the coastline plains of mud
Lie there for novelists to contemplate.

'All geography is exile, like the self.'
Is this the kind of thing they mean by 'late'?

Hans X arrived here for a single summer.
Nothing happened and he died
Still slim in his white suit at eighty,
Dry as this salt-shrunken table.
                                        The wind
Picks up across low dunes, the sun
Goes down like clockwork, like maritime commerce,
Red-eyed and unfinished, into the salt.
A fate we may suppose is anyone's.

*

Sleep is for sale, not to the sleepless only,
Reading on or staring out the clock,

But to the shallow generality as well.
Deep blankness makes them look like amateurs.

How soon the consolations of the lamp, the wakeful
Silence of the wide waste night, will seem perverse
And be forbidden!
                          Pale insomniacs,
Mark a final page and like your sleeping partners

Learn to die a little. Let the bones unfix,
The mind vacate its premises, until
Your absence feels like home, and you can reap
The dividend of all this quiet industry,
With two bright coppers on your empty eyes.

                          *

These complicated assignations
At provincial railway stations
And low convenient hotels
Complete with other people's smells
Mean 'public life is dead in X.'
Therefore they concentrate on sex,
Where it is always afternoon.
They say transgression sets them free:
They would have done it anyway.
She's always late. He comes too soon.
Although there is a price to pay,
What can outbid complicity
And sitting on a train all day?

*

A kind of poetry, a kind of sex,
Dreamed up by Stone-Age Protestants
(Have it by heart and keep it in your pants).
You can't imagine where you'll find it next
But rest assured it hasn't gone away.
Discovered down the back of a settee
Or scattered loosely on a table. Rita
Hayworth, I have come to set you free
From being classified as 'X'.
I am the President for life. My face
Is on the banknotes and my cheques
Are blanker than the bankrupt mind of God.
You'd like it really, Rita. Yes, you would.

*

Or the enormous range of afterwards,
The birchwoods and the endless marshes,
The grey sea and the greyer shore
Where you forget what drove you here.

Night falls. As one wave finishes
Another is preparing to arrive. The chalk roads
Turn to sand as economics vanishes.
This swamp was once a kingdom. We don't care.

We don't know from category error.
We just want to hate whoever's next –
Too rich, too philistine, too highly sexed.
The thing about the coast, it languishes.
Bring on the deluge and the reign of terror.

*

A yawning execution squad
Is mustered in the still-dark yard,
Unshaven and unbreakfasted
And for a moment hard to know
Apart from the condemned,
Who enter by another door,
A chorus of the unrehearsed
Who seem to have their roles by heart.
The difference you missed before
Is not the weapons only but the belts
That can hold up the trousers.

*It was a different world, my friend,
One inaccessible to bourgeois art.
Do not suppose effects have causes.*

*

Eternal afternoon, whose shadows play
Grandmother's footsteps as you look
Time in the face and quickly look away:
The clock examines you insatiably,
The moment of decision never ends.
Is this the prelude or the main event
And is the answer somewhere in a book,
Or will the signs be unmistakable
When you make history by being here,
Not there to hear the shouting on the stairs?
Is waiting in itself the true occasion,
And have you failed to rise to it so far,
And who exactly do you think you are?

*

Please stress the second syllable: e-*vil*,
When speaking of the hour that has come
That no one quite believed and no one doubted.

Grim glamour of its ordinariness!
It has the look you dream it will –
Street furniture, the lamp-posts' curlicues, heat-haze
On boulevards that have not been diverted –

At once like home and what you should not see,
The present, nothing more and nothing less,
Whose psychopathic citizens
May go abroad about their business,
Taking their cue from something in the air
To celebrate the end of days.

*

When all else fails, it must be murder.
The city's calm, with this in mind. The state
Will yield no other remedy. There is
A thirteenth hour, after all. The lime-trees
March in close formation to the gate
And then beyond into the Eastern haze.
Somewhere the final order is restored.
Knee-deep in our true element,
We catch the scent of blood and excrement
And the incinerated libraries
Of those who had it coming. We are home
In time to hear the cherry blossom
Thunder on the empty streets.

Do You Like Dickens?

You had a rival, that long-ago summer in Youghal,
The bookshop owner's creepy son with his funeral suit
And his dandruff, wringing his hands with lust
While she swam chastely up and down the pool.

All week you brooded on the manner of his death,
Until matters were brought to a head by her mother.
'So, Maurice, do you like Dickens?' 'Oh yes.' Creep creep.
'For example?' A pause. '. . . *A Christmas Carol*?' 'And?'

And off he crept. You knew there was a reason why
You took *Great Expectations* everywhere,
The night Estella came to find you in the outhouse.

You were a poor boy, a paperback, suitable
Only for poolside amusement. What did she call it?
The common pursuit: but she read you from cover to cover.

The Beautiful Librarians

The beautiful librarians are dead,
The fairly recent graduates who sat
Like Françoise Hardy's shampooed sisters
With cardigans across their shoulders
On quiet evenings at the issue desk,
Stamping books and never looking up
At where I stood in adoration.

Once I glimpsed the staffroom
Where they smoked and (if the novels
Were correct) would speak of men.
I still see the blue Minis they would drive
Back to their flats around the park,
To Blossom Dearie and red wine
Left over from a party I would never

Be a member of. Their rooms looked down
On dimming avenues of lime.
I shared the geography but not the world
It seemed they were establishing
With such unfussy self-possession, nor
The novels they were writing secretly
That somehow turned to 'Mum's old stuff'.

Never to even brush in passing
Yet nonetheless keep faith with them,
The ice-queens in their realms of gold –
It passes time that passes anyway.
Book after book I kept my word
Elsewhere, long after they were gone
And all the brilliant stock was sold.

Earlier Stuff

The earlier stuff. The later stuff.
Who but the author and his three
Best enemies would care or know
How to distinguish between them?
Life of the mind my arse. Life
Of swervy corridors, the *via minibara*.
Things to do in Spilsby when you're dead,
But that was in another county.
Life of the thin but earnest crowd
(*I'd like to thank you both for coming*).
And the hungover platform at dawn.
Life of the maximum stated dose
And then some. Of Bromsgrove, Leek,
Port Sunlight, Clitheroe, and grim Jock
Border towns where best forgotten
Incipodes . . . occurred. The earlier stuff.
Perhaps you'd rather leave it there?
Head of a fuckweasel journalist
Bounced off the sink in the hotel Gents
Till it broke – the sink, most likely.
The blood and chocolate early hours,
All that, all in the cause of *ard*, my friend.
If I were you. The dankness is all.
Nuneaton, Blubberhouses, Ingoldmells.
Ard of course was its own reward,
So not redeemable. You couldn't
Hand it back. You had to eat it.

Then or in the morning made
No odds; whenever, it would still
Be there, but hairier and stiff.
Ard vita. Dry like Ryvita.
Weevilled hardtack with salty grog,
All found and all, hélas, mislaid.
Grantham? Grantham. Rugeley, baby.
Take me oh take me to Pemmican Bay
For a year and a year and a year and a day.

Spilt Milk

I did not go to Hell when I was bought,
But like the planet merely kept on turning.

The business proved far simpler than I'd thought –
I was naïve. I'm learning.

You stare as though in shock, old friend.
If only it were up to me

We'd shake and you would understand
This virtuous necessity.

With all the factors in the case,
To keep my promise would have done no good:

I tell you this, and look you in the face,
And my betrayal turns to victimhood.

Old Lads at the Ramshill Hotel

The old lads, left for dead, once more arise
Through the velcro'd floor of the Family Lounge
To take their positively final leaves
Of the hard-faced ladies whose husbands they ignore.
Dancing again like good little navy-trained bantamweights,
The old lads are invoking a higher authority –
'Leave him, Stan, leave him' – by means of 'Spanish Eyes',
'Delilah', 'Never Can Say Goodbye' and they can't,
For this is the eternity of love
That opens the old lads' mouths 'like buckets to the skies'.
Ferocious and back-combed, the cackling ladies
Are all too aware of this game:
'You're a good turn, pet, but you're on too long',
Yet even their ironclad hearts, those *cold and lonely*
Lovely works of art, are still melted a half a degree
By these wobbly suitors with grease-grey quiffs
And suits which are older than they are, by gentlemen
Willing, more willing than Barkis, to take them
Away from this, as might an oriental potentate,
To the scarlet delights of the yashmaked seraglio
Or, to be practical, the carpark.
And when a gentleman – 'Not like you, eh, Stan' – a gentleman
Is crooning *The shadow of your smile when you are gone*
Will give us mucky dreams and light the dawwwwwwnnnnn, crooning
While perched on the glowing red tip of a last cigarette
Taken uninvited from a husband's open packet,
Crooning, an angel of fag-ash and old breath and pee-stains,
What lady can resist such old-school, old-world
Underwear-removing charm? – 'No, Stan, don't hit him, not yet.'

Lock-In

1.

The oiled-up model in the garage calendar
Slipped off that bonnet a long time back.
Married and divorced a time or two
She has invested in a café bar
As far from here as she can get.
South Shields, perhaps. Rodrigues. Reunion.
Somewhere your sort haven't fucked up yet.
You wonder what she actually deserved
When she let fall her pleasant guise, her thin array.
The jukebox mutters *Let's Get Wet*.
She has to bear the light of scrutiny
Forever or until they tear it down,
Whichever is the longer, fading a little
As they say they do, paler and further
As the years go by, as quick quick slow
As replays of *Amore*. Time to go,
But no one moves, since no one
Wants to miss the spirit draw
Or the Exotic who has commandeered
The Ladies. Hypocrite buveurs!

2.

There's been a funeral in the lounge
All day, the dead off the estate
Assembled to receive their own
With rich recrimination. You though
With your lives before you seem the last
To realize what's what, what's best,
To tell the signs from mere surroundings,
The figure from the ground, or if indeed
All this is only more periphrasis
Designed to tap a stranger, take the piss,
Or whether all these accidents are clues
To what there is when once you reach
The furthest annexe of the booze,
The Bower of Bliss and/or the Harpies' nest.

3.

You say you're only stopping for the one.
Come in and let the great world pass you by,
That figment all the regulars deny.
The tarred interior, the years,
The air of practised discontent
And simultaneous too late / not yet,
All passion, plus the wages, spent.
And bound to end in tears:
No need to wonder where they went –
Where else except in here
Whose ectoplasmic smoke and sweat
Alone appear to pay the rent?
In certain lights – a diving bell of malt,
A vodka tilting over the abyss of stout –
It has the flattering look of fate.
Eventually this is the place
That makes you long for ignorance again,
The one dim first-night room
An everywhere, a treasure-cave of alibis
And home to forty thieves
And their transactions: *blue pills, mek yer*
Spill yer muck all night, which leaves
Precisely nothing to be said, and all
Eternity to say it to the dead.

Daylight Saving

The clocks go back. As the light fails
Down on the path by the Metro line
Where yellow leaves have drifted overnight
Against the wire fences, men walk with dogs
To show they are not murderers.
Neither here nor there, trains pass
On other lines. They pull the grey air
Inside out. The dog spooks easily,
Knowing what humans will do.

I stop to listen where there used to be
A house you couldn't find except on foot.
The kids demolished it, and creepers claim
Its blackened bricks. The smell
Of years-old burning makes me homeless,
But the story is not mine, no more
Than this unhappy accident of place
That lies beyond a frontier no one drew
And yet stands undisputed. Here

At world's end, nothing intervenes,
And if a place could know me, now it does.
A step too far, beyond the light
Shed by the streetlamp at the bridge
And things are what they are, dark air
And ruination, far-off trains, the dog
Who, like his foolish master,
Cannot tell which way to turn.
Invite me in, then, emptiness.

The Wendigo

i.m. Douglas Houston

You would have recognized this place,
The path that runs beside the Metro, walked
By sober adults and their upright dogs
But turning into bandit country
Now the nights draw in at just gone three.
The wire fences like the ones at school
Seem placed to emphasize the ragged edge
Of a forsaken order we affected to despise –
Mundane municipalities that could afford
To house and feed our discontent. No more.
Where once the Wild Wood grew, the in-between
Emerges as a bleak and Badgerless republic,
Hawthorn scrub and sycamore, and on a lost
Allotment bordering a siding and a tunnel
Fireweed staggers on like wild white-headed Lears.
You would have understood this place
Speaks only with itself, and yet have tried
To overhear the rumour of the shoaling leaves
And cider-bottles, rutted earth and Durex
And, concealed among the red-raw docks,
Discreet excreta of the (canine?) bourgeoisie.
What does it say, this nightfall then, with
Everyone indoors or meant to be, as darkness
Takes possession of the ground once more

Or waits impatiently beyond the flickering rim
Of failing streetlight? You must know by now.
There comes the howl of the disconsolate
Exurban Wendigo, who cannot be appeased
By knowing he does not exist. Ah Wendigo,
The case is worse for those who must be real.

AntiMcGuffin

Precise and mad, the one that nails it
Must be in there somewhere. – Otherwise.
The pages turn politely, neutral
Like the staff of the hotel. If that were so
Then now you'd turn the register around
For them to check it too. Quite soon
Without your even asking they would call
The manager, who'd call the owner, after which
A priest, the police and men with nets
Would gather in the car-park silently.

But all of that is some way off as yet.
Keep looking, since you have your life
Before you, and the evening foyer still seems
Young enough for dreaming of the truth.
The heavy pages turn discreetly,
Receptionists and porters crowding near,
And cleaners who speak little English,
Hoping for the best when hope is gone,
While showing the respect that this derangement
Surely merits. Somewhere here's the thing

You have in mind. – Since otherwise. More nods.
– There is a river and a street that runs downhill
Towards it from Ohio, creaking jetties,
Boats just now embarked, with hazard lights
That vanish slowly in the fog. Of course.
But that by no means does it justice, and the page
Does not appear. Of course. Meanwhile
The foyer and the corridors extend
Immensely in the dark beneath dark lamps
That as you speak are one by one extinguished.

Lamplight

'and say then, that was my life'
Derek Mahon, 'J. P. Donleavy's Dublin'

Under the lamp-light the stiff hand moves,
Over the page and the next,
As though this must be liberty, this
Early retirement into the text –
Black marks against the column of the day,
The week-to-view, the month, the year,
The hand moving on and the clock's hands
Turning backward in the mirror.
All, all, as was foretold
When the old lady stood in her doorway, smiling
And shading her blind eyes, one evening in June,
In the porch in the shade of the chestnuts, the evening
Extending, extending, the late sun
Held in the chestnuts' branches, the taxi
Standing at the kerb. And this was not the last of it,
Not quite, not quite – so wait and see,
As she would tell the child that once you were:
Hold on and never give an inch before
The time, which you will recognize.
She turned, went in and closed the door
Against the ordinary sunlit evening, one of many
We had watched together neutrally, like gods
Who know their duty and like company,

Remembering, remembering, among the dim grave-goods,
The paintings and the furniture, the photographs
Of mother, father, sisters, brother
All long gone and yet as though
Still living somewhere else forever,
Held in those grey gardens and demolished terraces,
Relying on the witness borne
By those who know them to be dead, who find
That time forbids us to perpetually mourn,
But wait here still when everything is said.

Residential Brownjohnesque

For A. B.

They've put you in the Edward Thomas Room,
The dim one in the annexe with the tiny window blocked by leaves,
With a sleepless chiffchaff and the bed
You realize eventually is coffin-shaped.
There will be baked potatoes and a sense of déjà vu,
Lasagne and, perhaps, a sense of déjà vu.
The Director is on leave / is leaving / has left /
Is barricaded in the office with
A shotgun and a box of Mini Cheddars.
It all seems very far away, The Rurals,
Like somewhere you're not really meant to go,
Not liking smells, or sheep especially, in Wales almost.
Yet after all, what is it? Only a week of your life,
One long week of the short third act,
In which to have fallen with a sense of déjà vu
Among demons and maniacs and bores.
Reading down the list of names,
You seem to know them all from somewhere –
Flanerie O'Anaconda, Delphine Stain,
Euphemia Bandersnatch, Clive Overbite
And the indomitable Norman Shouty,
And someone who is always not there yet
But on a train / a plane / a mission / medication / sectioned.
And all the rest. How many of the bastards are there? They are waiting.

If the slurry served at dinner seems to have a fringe on top
Remember, truth is beauty, beauty truth
And that is all you need to know. So eat your greens.
Enough of this, it's time, it's time.
There is a further room prepared, the Déjà Room,
Down a dark path, through a mire, a grimpen, a minefield, a boneyard,
Wales, not far,
And there at last you have to talk to them. They're waiting,
Waiting with their pens, their grudges and their daggers, eagerly.

Dialogue in the Multi-Function Room

For Joachim Sartorius

When they announced we'd 'wrestle with the truth'
It seems they meant it literally,
So that while we are in China, it is also
Batley Corn Exchange at 4pm
One winter Saturday in 1964, which means
This is eternity. Kent Walton commentates.
One in, one out: as Kendo Nagasaki leaves,
So Billy Two Rivers flies in from the ropes.
When words give place to image, sense
To its performance, afternoon
To thirsty dusk, and Johnny Kwango
High fives evil Mick McManus, can it be
That I alone grow weary of a sport
That everybody knows is fixed?
Two falls or a submission to the
Ineluctable forces of history –
A phone call, the need for a piss,
The summons to drill in the hot white square
Beneath the oompah shouting-music.

What is our subject? That is the question.
Let us turn grotesque disparities
Between distinct symbolic orders to
Rhetorical advantage. Tear his effing head off.

How I hate culture! Yet I do my part –
For did not Ovid in his exile learn
To pass the time enduring Boston Crabs
And forearm smashes from the Thracian
Mat-men of Constanta, grapple-fans?
Seeing how the world must end
In spectacle, with blood and sand?
Although not yet. I rise and limp
Through sunset while the dialogue
Rages and thuds in the cross-arts shed.
There is an avenue of plane-trees,
Twisted like the Wood of Wrestling Suicides,
Where everybody smokes their phones
And screams inaudibly and then goes back
To put their sweaty trunks on. *Und so weiter.*

Mutatis Mutandis

The steersman is lost and the hole he has made
In the water has swallowed his cry and healed over.
The curious fishes must make what they can
From his bones, or the great whale may vomit him up
On the shore, at the feet of a queen who stands
Waiting and waiting through moon after moon
With no news and no rumours but only her sorrow
For company. Maritime cities are burned
To the waterline, plague passes north
Like an army of phantoms by night, and volcanoes
Roar out from pole to equator, while the stones of the world
Break open and swallow each other, and darkness
Closes over the face of the water, and new seas arise
From the wreckage of empires, and settle, and still.

At the third stroke the time will be nothing at all,
The time of un-dreaming, when rivers and language
Are locked in the ice, when the eye and the ear have grown
Weary of seeing and hearing. The play and the music are over.
The desert gives way to the desert and heaven's high quarrels
Have found a new venue. The gods never speak of us.
We must wake into this poisoned sleep and gather
Our rag-and-bone birthright about us and wait
Until somebody hears herself talking and says it again
And somebody beats on a drum with the bone of an aurochs
And finds that the rhythm becomes an opinion
And then with the same bone sketches a line in the sand

As the blizzards melt back to the poles and a fire is lit
That all men will know of, and worship, or fear.

So many waves of desire, dynasties, fetishes,
Novel barbarians out of the inexhaustible East.
Inquisitors are always on their way, and at one time
All this was just fields, where the cemeteries grow
From the bones of the infantry, forests of marble
In which we may seek after wisdom, pursuing
The fugitive spirit of things as it slips through the silent
Ranks of those King Death conscripted for a host
The like of which has not been seen by men or gods —
And in whose vanguard, Goddess, you and I both ride
With fire and sword, because it must be so:
The ocean and the mountain and the fire at the core
Demand it. Why else do we lay siege once more to Troy
Or Carthage, or whatever this place will be called?

Antistrophe: Underwater Fires

As we know, there are submarine fires –
Vents in the sea-bed, like stony syringes, like flare-stacks
In the upper world, doing the work
With a steady efficiency, voiding and voiding
Black flame into darkness. Beware of analogy,
That's what they say, or they used to:
Father McMahon, who used to coach boxing, remember,
Was keen to remind us: keep up your guard, boys:
The world is the world, not a figure of speech.

What we witness down there in the visible dark
Is the working of nature, and therefore – and therefore
The bell rings for break in the lecture-room scene
Where weary Professor Zybulski dismisses
The callow and somnolent boys and girls
With a brusque affection they will recognize
All too late, when they suffer unwarranted incineration
By strange un-American fountains of flame
In the carpark. It's not rocket science.

The murderers wait discreetly to one side,
While Professor Zybulski removes his thick glasses
And pinches the bridge of his nose. He would show us
The true cost of knowledge. He walks to the car.
It is night now. The murderous chauffeurs exhibit
A paranoid calm that has no need of language, until
– *The Professor is here, Mr President. – Show him in, Murph.*

The president too is a man, as his spectacles prove.
– *We need you at the centre of the earth by Tuesday.*

The Professor, long divorced by cruel science,
Goes for dinner with his daughter, the ethical
Corporate lawyer. *You promised me, Daddy. You promised me*
You wouldn't pierce the mantle any more. Does that
Mean nothing? Zybulski examines a dry crust of bread
As though to use it to explain the structure of the world.
The waiter comes. Zybulski shakes his head.
The daughter stands. *I'm pregnant. – Who's the father?*
– *He's a giant reptile, Daddy – but you wouldn't care about that.*

As you grow older, it's harder to care what you miss
When you have to go out for a leak. You come back.
And they're talking a different language. It's finished,
Job done and done over, the final combustion
Blazing away till there comes the impossible end,
Black silence across the deep bed, black afterwards –
Nothing is happening, nothing is over –
The President's words were a figure of speech –
And nothing beginning, world without end, Amen.

Three Frivolous Poems

The Different Rilke at Stalag Luft X

– It's been a good year for the roses.
– Ja, but for you the war is over.

Sorrows of the Voivode

People think it's easy
Being a voivode. Let me tell you.
Bring me a loggerhead. Not that one.

Haiku as the Work of the Evil One

First you give me all
Your money, then I give you
This old rope for free.

Protocols of the Superfluous Immortal

A god long since retired to the seaside
Checks the post and tuts at the barometer.
Some dirty weather in the offing —

Freighters in the Channel battened down,
The green wave-walls remote and terrifying as his youth.
He re-reads Hornblower in bed. He never sleeps.

An egg, please, and *The Telegraph*.
His constitutional, the bandstand,
Out along the pier; the wintry courtesies

Accorded others of his solitary kind.
Then afternoon. No weather worth the name.
The day extends towards whatever

It extends towards, forever, and the god
Applies himself once more to thirteen down,
The only word that rhymes with breath. But it's no good.

The Actuary

'. . . *we concede that the figure is all imagination . . . we say that*
it has not the slightest meaning for us, except for its nobility . . .
We recognize it perfectly. We do not realize it.'
Wallace Stevens, 'The Noble Rider and the Sound of Words'

Great actuary of the imagined thing,
It is to you we turn at last. Too long
Among the unrealities, you say,
Aboard the chariot, the passage of divinity
Across the heavens, all of that.

Now we have spent their force and ours.
We sink once more towards the earth
That we imagine we remember,
All too late, since we are changed
As earth is changed in our neglect.

There will be nothing of the plain estate
For which our dreaming may atone, no love
Sufficient to the cause. There will be
Time alone, that we did not create
And cannot hold us as we fall.

Nobody's Uncle

'*That's one old man who's nobody's uncle.*'
Douglas Dunn

His wallet will contain no photographs
Of grandkids or the harbours he re-entered
Under shellfire, bringing off the wounded.
The lottery's completely passed him by.
On chairs in shady doorways shelling peas,
Tilting up their faces to the sunset,
No girls grown old think fondly of him now.
They find him hard to place. They go inside.
At dusk he might be taken for a fisherman
Who sets out more from habit than belief,
A final wild-haired independent, dressed
In such authentic salt-stiff rags and stooped
So anciently among his stinking gear
You might suspect that someone's made him up.
Suppose you stop to pass the time,
He sees straight through, with the impersonal
Assurance of a beast or of a god.
So here you are.
                    And when you step aboard
The shore will slip behind
So swiftly you'll be there before you know.

Wedding Breakfast

Here is the present we know as forever. Here in the street
Beyond the open café door, it is snowing again
In the dark, a gift for the morning. No one must see.
If anybody does, it is Mme la Concierge
Across the way, behind her barricaded porte-cochère.
But nothing has changed in the stench of her simmering bones
In the stairwell. If one of the tenants should open a window
To take in a breath of blue ice, then hold it like the pause
Before the down-stroke of the baton wakes the orchestra
And understand this paradise too soon,
Then that is none of her concern, Monsieur. She did not
Make this world, and those who choose to dwell in it
Must find their own salvation. *Here, amid the snow, Madame,*
The rendezvous of yesteryear and evermore? She cannot say,
But as for her she has her work, and hopes that you have yours.

Along the snowy quai a girl in next to nothing types a novel,
Indifferent to the crisis she provokes in her admirers
By resting the machine against her skin and ordering
Its regiment of tiny metal hooves into a trot,
Then from a canter to a charge. It is magnificent
But is it literature, or something else more interesting?
She shivers, she basks, and then with a tiny furious foot
Grinds out her cigarette. Intolerable happiness
Of merely being there to witness her put on her face,
Her stockings and her wide straw hat, as she gives
Her consent to go boating, no matter the run on the banks,

No matter the blizzard, the shellbursts, the plague. *No,*
I shall never marry. Or only the once. Is that the time? Row faster!
No matter. Our lady the city is perfect forever.

Here is the wedding in the snow, the locals joining in
Because their happiness is naturally required as well.
The party cross the street to the café – the sudden friends,
The bride who wears her gown of snow
Like a platonic nakedness, the groom deranged
By his good fortune, commanding every glass be raised,
And glad to see the chimney sweep who brings
His prophecy of happiness on happiness
To the exalted monochrome of this eternal Now,
The white city, the ghost of itself in the snow-fog, laid bare
For a moment, the sleepwalking river too perfect.
So here they are at last, the bride and Death, for this is not
A chimney sweep, but, now we see, the coalman.
See, impossible, the dark companion downs his glass
And stoops to reach into his grimy sack, to show the bride –
This too is forever, forever and ever, amen,
Impossible, impossible – a serpent from the mine.

At the Solstice

We say *Next time we'll go away.*
But then the winter happens, like a secret

We've to keep yet never understand,
As daylight turns to cinema once more:

A lustrous darkness deep in ice-age cold,
And the print in need of restoration

Starting to consume itself
With snowfall where no snow is falling now.

Or could it be a cloud of sparrows, dancing
In the bare hedge that this gale of light

Is seeking to uproot? Let it be sparrows, then,
Still dancing in the blazing hedge,

Their tender fury and their fall,
Because it snows, because it burns.

Long Wave

Whether you stay or go, you hear
The water brushing at the threshold
And the long wave comes and carries you –
Home, home, as far as far,
The compass gathered like a rose
Into its bud, till you are neither
Here nor there, or so you almost know
At dusk and dawn, when time's the only praise
That counts, outsailing its creator.
When the melancholy wave withdraws
Into a patience you can never share,
For half a day and half eternity you wish
To leave yourself marooned and calling
From the shore, until the long wave comes
Climbing past death's stony door again
And spilling over till it seems
Like something you might know, but is a wave,
And not the first word or the last,
Home, home, as far as far,
The compass gathered like a rose.

Grey Rose

When you enter grey rose country,
After the days, more days, the last,
The comfortless finality
That has not finished yet, the rest
Versus the rest, no aftermath
Is absolute enough for death.
Grey roses' petals do not fall
At summer's end: the grey rose rears
Its hydra heads to stand for all
That can be neither mourned nor shed
In the grey gardens of the dead.
Grey roses worn on the lapel,
Grey roses rooted in the mind,
Grey roses with a sweet-sick smell,
Grey roses, grey with all regret
For all that has not happened yet.
The grey rose has no history
In the lost world it imitates.
The grey rose is and cannot be.
It neither toils nor spins. It waits,
A truth that will not set you free,
Grey rose that's nothing but a rose
That flowers here where nothing grows.

Café de l'imprimerie

I wait for you inside a glass beside
The long dim window of the Café de l'Imprimerie.
I see you, beautiful and wry

And not yet here, and yet not here,
While this late summer evening never ends
And never ends but is infinitesimally

Dimming on the street beside Les Halles where I
Can see you, beautiful and wry as you draw near,
And I am reassured you are not coming. Yes.

All night I wait for you at the Café de l'Imprimerie.
Your absence makes you beautiful and wry
And this late summer evening never ends,

Nor does the beautiful intolerable
Music, where the truth is cut
With sentiment and surely fatal.

Come now. Do not come. Come now. Do not,
And lead me to a room where you undress,
A bare white room at an untraceable address

Where we will stay forever. Come now. Do not. Yes.

The Lost of England

Forgive me, England. As so often I was dreaming
On a train that drowsed along, cross-country
By the insane route that takes the reason prisoner.

A pile of scripts lay on the table, nagging with their claims
To cross the boundary between 2.1 and First,
And so I had my life before me and I dreamed.

The journey too conspired to evade: somewhere at hand
Lay cities we would never visit, and instead we seemed
To slow continually inside the rainy summer heat

Through nowhere much, that might have been the Midlands
And might not, past nameless settlements and cooling towers,
Chains of ponds, canals where nothing moved, low hills

I'd never walk but knew were sacred to the childhoods
Of the unknown and the invisible, who seemed to wait
There in the wings of that unceasing afternoon as though

Our going were a signal to resume their secret lives.
I didn't sleep, and yet at times I woke as we ran slowly
Through a cutting in the chalk or into woodland thick with shade,

And once again the Hardy–Housman essay caught my gaze,
So full of promise and so unfulfilled, and then I fell
Between the lines into the text, to where my double did

The living and the talking, and he said, 'Another day,
Another train, another overset examiner, and this
Unwillingness to come down off the fence might well

Have signalled the Creation to unwrite itself and be
Resolved once more into the immanent electric dew
That has no origin, the anti-clock by which the sweep-hands

Of the fleeing galaxies are set. But luckily or not,
It means instead that I arrived where I have always been,
Within the central wood among the trees, at walking pace,

With oak and ash behind the birches' airy masts, the rumour
Of a storm dispelled, and rain expected, and the leaves
Flirtatious in the sudden breeze. This was the secret county

That resigned itself before its title was removed
From wayside stones and letter-heads, before the light
From dusty platform awnings ceased to fall exactly as

It fell before the spinster with her anxious bags
And gangs of boatered schoolgirls parked on trunks –
All waiting for the slow connection from one decade

To another in the Long Mid-Century – all looked away
And then dissolved, and there was neither light nor dark
But somewhere that had never been, a high-hedged crossroads

In a fold of hills, a sawn-off fingerpost, and barrels
Full of concrete placed to block the road in case. In case of what?
A van might come, a solitary horseman at a walk,

Yet neither would. In case of what? Enquiries are closed:
Out of this place desire not to go. In case of what?
In case you should be witness to the marriage of the real

And the imagined, the irrevocable state that none
Has yet returned to speak about. To satisfy your wish
Would cost you everything, not all of which is yours to give.

Then rather witness while you can this small infinity –
Its signal boxes, sidings deep in dock and campion,
Brick station houses shuttered in the pressing heat,

A timber-yard, a ragged hawthorn lane where caravans
Pretend they have not been discovered yet, with horses tied
To sleepers on the rutted verge, more woods, a road

Beneath the railway bridge, more woods, a half-mown hillside,
Sheds, allotments, barrows propped on end – the whole misfigured
Fact of things that you can neither touch nor live without,

This green reserve where no one comes or goes and all
Are necessary as the weather, and where no one seeks
Coherence greater than this afternoon suggests, and where

To all intents and purposes the living and the dead may pass
Their time beneath a sun in cloudy splendour. Listen here:
Imagine, then, by miracle, with me, that evening comes

Eventually along a street that you have glimpsed and lost.
You hear unseasonable fireworks and smell the smoke of bonfires
In the hidden gardens, and know that there are people running

In back lanes and riding bikes and gazing up as if this night
Must mark a great but never-named arrival. See now, moon and stars,
To which the smoke and flames agreeably ascend. It is

A secret. You will never see the faces, hear the voices,
Live as they live, speak to them, or wish as they wish
Simply to be there, but – who knows why? – you come to witness

What they love and are, and reach for what cannot be touched
Or owned, and learn to love the lost of England.'
Then we stopped and I awoke. This looked like Crewe, the ruined

Temple at the heart of things, and I began to read again.

Passage for New Holland

The place would tell you if it could,
And that will never happen, but it might.
The silence feeds upon itself. The words
Dictate themselves in white on white.
The ragged fields becoming hawthorn woods.
Moonrise. Quarries. Estuary at dusk.

Think of a number. Forty years.
The casualties. The weather. Light
Falling on the water and the page,
The ferry coming in and going out.
Will not, may not, will not, never.
Those whom etc let none dissever.

The ragged pastoral grows picturesque
With too much looking. *You are here*:
Regard this penance as a privilege.
The meantime is imperious:
It would not read a line you wrote.
The tide has risen, just like that.

Lovers and the dead will not
Persuade it to release a single anecdote,
And yet the craving for a sign
Converts the slightest pretext to a rite.
Be faithful? How could you be otherwise?
Be faithful, then. Here comes the night.

Where it Comes From

A sleeping commune in a far
Département, a village the ignored
Canal ignores in passing.
The bar is never open
And the church is always shut
And no one seems to know
The names of those far hills
That stand so promisingly black
Against the slate-blue sky.
For instance. And within
This final province is a room
With pen and paper on a table
At the window, left,
It would appear, for someone else,
Who has to understand
What you can only love.